Maple Press
2.95

D0569064

July 2005

PRIMARY SOURCES OF REVOLUTIONARY
SCIENTIFIC DISCOVERIES AND THEORIES™

MENDELEYEV AND THE PERIODIC TABLE

KATHERINE WHITE

rosen central
Primary Source™

The Rosen Publishing Group, Inc., New York

Published in 2005 by The Rosen Publishing Group, Inc.
29 East 21st Street, New York, NY 10010

Copyright © 2005 by The Rosen Publishing Group, Inc.

First Edition

Library of Congress Cataloging-in-Publication Data

White, Katherine (Katherine G.)
Mendeleyev and the periodic table / by Katherine White.
    p. cm. — (Primary sources of revolutionary scientific discoveries and theories series)
Includes bibliographical references and index.
ISBN 1-4042-0310-9 (library binding)
1. Chemists—Russia (Federation)—Biography. 2. Chemical elements.
[DNLM: 1. Mendeleyev, Dmitry Ivanovich, 1834–1907. 2. Chemistry, Physical—Biography. 3. Periodicity. WZ 100 M5375w 2004]
I. Title. II. Series.
QD22.M43W45 2004
540'.92—dc22

                                                                    2004011248

Printed in Hong Kong

On the front cover: A photograph of Dmitry Mendeleyev working at an office in Moscow, Russia, in 1904

On the back cover: Top to bottom: Nicolaus Copernicus, Charles Darwin, Edwin Hubble, Johannes Kepler, Gregor Mendel, Dmitry Mendeleyev, Isaac Newton, James Watson *(right)* and Francis Crick *(left)*

CONTENTS

INTRODUCTION

From the time Dmitry Mendeleyev was a young boy, he loved science. His passion for the subject began as a love for physics, but he eventually built his career studying and researching chemistry. Mendeleyev's love for science was his deepest passion. It was his passion for chemistry that guided him to one of the greatest scientific achievements of the nineteenth century—the periodic table of elements.

THE DREAM THAT SHOOK THE WORLD

In 1869, while working on the second volume of his groundbreaking book *The Principles of Chemistry*, Mendeleyev became entranced with how to group the elements—the basic building blocks of the universe. Mendeleyev had written the first volume over the course of four years, but he planned to write the first three chapters of the second volume in just four days. After three days of continuous work without any sleep, Mendeleyev knew he was close to completing the third chapter and was also about to uncover a huge discovery. Then, during a quick nap, the periodic table of elements appeared to him in a dream. Later he recalled his experience that afternoon:

> *"I saw in a dream a table where all the elements fell into place as required. Awakening, I immediately wrote it down on a piece of paper."*

Few minds have contributed as much to science as the mind of Dmitry Mendeleyev. While young Dmitry was considered slow, his mind developed rapidly. By the time he was a young adult, he was considered brilliant. In college, he began publishing papers that challenged the scientific world. This photograph, taken in 1905, captures the chemist near the end of his life. By this time, Mendeleyev's groundbreaking periodic table of elements had been accepted and was implemented in nearly every classroom and laboratory around the world. Mendeleyev's work would lead directly to the discovery of subatomic particles, DNA, and a better understanding of the universe.

Today, the periodic table is still considered one of the greatest inventions in the field of chemistry. The periodic table is used in nearly every science laboratory, book, and classroom throughout the world. The creation of the periodic table makes Mendeleyev one of the greatest scientists of all time, placing his achievement on the same scale as Joseph Priestley's (1733-1804) discovery of oxygen, Albert Einstein's (1879-1955) theory of relativity, and Charles Darwin's (1809-1882) theory of evolution. Read on to find out how Mendeleyev's passion for chemistry led him to the discovery of the periodic table of elements.

CHAPTER 1

On February 8, 1834, Dmitry Ivanovich Mendeleyev was born to his proud parents, Ivan and Marya Mendeleyev. (Mendeleyev is sometimes spelled "Mendeleev" because of the way the Russian language is translated into English.) Born with blond hair and blue eyes, Mendeleyev was the youngest of fourteen or seventeen children—no one knows for sure the exact number. Mendeleyev's mother gave birth to him in Tobolsk, a town that lies in a vast and remote region of Russia called Siberia. The town was home to many generations of Mendeleyev's family, especially on his mother's side, the Kornilievs. The Korniliev family introduced some very important businesses to the people of Siberia. Fifty years earlier, Mendeleyev's grandfather started the first newspaper in the history of Siberia. He was also well-known for his paper and glass factories called Korniliev Glass.

A GENIUS'S EARLY YEARS

Tragedy Strikes

Soon after Mendeleyev's birth, Ivan went blind. Before losing his sight, Ivan was the director of the local school. However, his blindness forced him to resign. Ivan had always been the provider for his family, but now his sudden blindness forced

As the youngest child, young Dmitry was favored by his mother, who provided him with as many opportunities as possible. However, Mendeleyev's childhood was also riddled with catastrophe. Both his father and sister died while he was very young, and his mother was forced to raise the entire Mendeleyev family. This photograph captures Mendeleyev as a young man, around the time he first enrolled at the Central Pedagogic Institute in St. Petersburg, Russia. By 1853, Mendeleyev's mother and sister would die from tuberculosis. Without a family, Mendeleyev found solace in science, his passion. The world of science was rapidly changing, and young Dmitry would play an integral role in bringing science into the twentieth century and beyond.

Mendeleyev's mother, Marya, to support their large family. Luckily, Marya was a smart, determined, and very open-minded woman for the times. Back then, most women were in charge of running the household and expected their husbands to support the family. Not Marya. She was not overwhelmed by the idea of heading off to work every day. Instead, she began to manage one of her father's glass factories in order to bring in income to support her family. Some of Mendeleyev's first memories are of going with his mother to the Korniliev Glass factory in Aremziansk, a small village about twenty miles (thirty-two kilometers) from Tobolsk. There, young Dmitry spent his days playing with the factory workers' children.

Early School Years

In the early years of his schooling, Dmitry was not very excited about his studies. He rarely paid attention, and his poor grades showed his lack of enthusiasm. The only areas of school in which Dmitry excelled were math and science. Dmitry was especially interested in physics, the study of matter, motion, energy, and force. Unfortunately, Dmitry's school focused much more on older subjects, such as Greek and Latin, and not on more cutting-edge subjects like science.

His Family's Support

Dmitry's family wanted to support his love for science, so Marya invited her son to visit the glass factory as often as he liked. There, Mendeleyev learned all about glass and glassblowing. Glass is really just a mixture of sand, soda, lime, and a lot of heat. Dmitry enjoyed learning about the scientific side of glassblowing, such as how much heat was needed to make glass. He was especially interested in how all the separate ingredients, when mixed together, became

COMMON TERMS USED IN PHYSICS

energy The ability of a system to do work. For example, your body is a system that does work, so you have energy.

force A "push" or "pull" experienced by a mass.

matter Anything that takes up space or has mass. (Mass is the measure of the amount of matter.)

motion The movement of objects or matter from place to place.

an entirely new substance. Mendeleyev's deep interest in how glass is made shows his initial interest in chemistry.

Dmitry's brother-in-law, Bessargin, was also a big influence on the boy's education. Bessargin was a political rebel who played a role in the uprising in Russia called the 1825 December Revolution, which was staged by a political group called the Decembrists. The group wanted Russia to change to a constitutional government, and establish some form of democratic government. When the revolution failed, Russian officials sentenced the leaders of the revolution to death and banished the rest of the Decembrists to Siberia. Bessargin was one of the exiles sent to Siberia; this is where he met and married Dmitry's sister Olga. Noticing that Dmitry's grades were bad, Bessargin began tutoring young Dmitry. Bessargin was also very interested in science, so both student and teacher would read and talk about science for hours on end.

Learning the Ropes

By the time he turned thirteen, Dmitry's grades had greatly improved. In fact, they improved so much that everyone began to notice his remarkable intelligence. Dmitry's teachers said he had a great mind for science. He would finish his school day, go home, and conduct all kinds of scientific experiments. Soon, everyone agreed: Dmitry was brilliant.

As the youngest child, Dmitry spent an enormous amount of time with his mother. Over the years, the two developed a strong relationship. Marya favored Dmitry because she always believed he would become a great success. When Marya saw how much Dmitry loved science, she vowed her son would someday go on to study at a very important university. Marya's dream was to be able to pay for her son's education.

Loss and Conflict

In 1840, the Mendeleyev family went through two sudden tragedies. Each one struck the family in a deeply personal way. When Dmitry's father passed away in 1848, the whole family grieved. Then, in that same year, the glass factory burned to the ground. The tragedies left Marya alone and without any way to support her two youngest children. Marya gathered Dmitry and his older sister Liza and moved the family to Moscow, a major city in Russia.

The 1,300-mile (2,092 km) journey was long and hard. Marya was more than fifty years old, but she was convinced that Moscow offered better opportunities for her children. Upon arriving in Moscow, her hope was challenged when Dmitry was not accepted into any schools. He was not turned down for lack of intelligence. The only reason he was turned down was because of old rules in Moscow's educational system in which children from Siberia, who were considered lower class, were not accepted as students. Marya was heartbroken, but still she did not lose sight of her goal. Instead, she moved the family another 400 miles (644 km) to St. Petersburg, then the capital of Russia, where Dmitry was accepted into a school on a full scholarship.

Tragedy Strikes Again and Again

Within just a few months of the family's arrival in St. Petersburg in 1850, Mendeleyev's mother contracted tuberculosis, also called TB, which was a very deadly illness common in the mid-1800s. Dmitry's mother remained strong even though she knew she was dying. According to *Mendeleyev's Dream: The Quest for the Elements*, by Paul Strathern, Marya's dying words to Mendeleyev

St. Petersburg was a bustling hub of culture and industry—a far cry from Mendeleyev's childhood home in Siberia. In St. Petersburg, Mendeleyev's mind flourished at the Central Pedagogic Institute. For someone who grew up in a barren and remote land, the big city would foster Mendeleyev's longing to challenge institutions, such as Russia's lagging scientific community that was far behind that of the rest of the world. This photo captures a busy street in St. Petersburg in the late nineteenth century.

were, "Refrain from illusions, insist on work and not on words. Patiently seek divine and scientific truth." Thirty years later, Mendeleyev quoted his mother's words in a scientific paper, which he dedicated to her.

Within a year, Dmitry's sister Liza also died from tuberculosis. In 1853, Dmitry was also diagnosed with the disease. Doctors told Dmitry he had only a few months to live. It was Dmitry's third year at the Central Pedagogic Institute, and already he was starting to build a good name. He was known as a devoted science student, and many of his professors thought he was truly gifted.

Even though he was sick, Dmitry still pursued his studies. If anything, he was even more devoted. While he was forced to spend a lot time in bed, Dmitry was studying science whenever he wasn't resting. At the time, Dmitry was moving away from his initial interest in physics and was beginning to concentrate much more on chemistry. Chemistry is the study of matter and the changes that take place within that matter.

During the mid-1800s, the science world began to turn its attention toward chemistry. Many scientists were beginning to discover new elements. Each new element provided another piece to our puzzling universe. Elements are the building blocks of all life. They make up everything in our universe.

COMMON TERMS USED IN CHEMISTRY

atom The smallest particle of an element that can exist either alone or in combination.

compound A substance formed by two or more elements.

elements The basic building blocks of all matter; substances that cannot be broken down into simpler substances through ordinary chemistry.

molecule The smallest particle of a substance that retains all the properties of the substance and is composed of more than one atom.

states of matter All the material on earth is in one of three states: solid, liquid, or gas.

In order for Dmitry to stay in school, his friends brought assignments to his bedside where he worked while resting in bed. Eventually, Dmitry even ventured out and began going to the school's laboratory to work on his own experiments. He would return to his bed, exhausted, and write up his experiments before falling asleep. By the time he was twenty, Dmitry was publishing articles on his own experiments. His first article, published in a science journal in 1854, was called "Chemical Analysis of a Sample from Finland." Publishing an article in a well-respected science journal was a huge accomplishment for such a young scientist.

Student of the Year Heads Off to Teach

In 1855, Dmitry earned great recognition when he was given the Student of the Year Award by the Central Pedagogic Institute. This was a great honor that Dmitry deserved. Along with the award, Dmitry also received a teaching position. His first teaching post was on the Crimean Peninsula at a school in Simferopol. The Crimean Peninsula lies to the south of Russia and is partially surrounded by the Black Sea. Unfortunately, when Mendeleyev arrived there, the Crimean War (1853–1856) was in full swing. The Crimean War was fought over religious freedoms between Russia and an alliance of the United Kingdom, France, and the Ottoman Empire. Most of the fighting happened on the Crimean Peninsula, so the entire region was in shambles, and the school had been closed for months. Dmitry found himself poor and living in a war-torn region.

The Doctor Is In

Even though Dmitry thought his journey to the Crimean Peninsula turned out to be worthless, it really turned out to be a

The Crimean War lasted three years and ravaged parts of southern Russia. After all the hardships he overcame during his childhood and young adulthood, Mendeleyev's first teaching job was dashed due to nations fighting on the Crimean Peninsula. This painting captures the bloody Battle of the Alma (September 20, 1854), in which the Russians were crushed by the British and French armies.

life-changing event. About one month after his arrival, Dmitry learned that his tuberculosis was misdiagnosed, meaning he was not really sick with the life-threatening disease. The news spurred Dmitry into action. He left the peninsula and headed back to St. Petersburg to take on the science world, one experiment at a time.

CHAPTER 2

A YOUNG SCIENTIST STUDIES AND GROWS

In 1856, Mendeleyev arrived back in St. Petersburg ready to begin his scientific career. When he was twenty-two, Mendeleyev landed a teaching position at the prestigious St. Petersburg University. This was a remarkable accomplishment for such a young man. At the university, Mendeleyev's teaching schedule blended perfectly with his work. A few days a week, he would give lectures on chemistry, with the remainder of the week open so he could perform experiments using the school's laboratories.

At this point in his career, Mendeleyev was fast becoming an expert in the world of chemistry. He would constantly read about the latest chemistry discoveries in journals and books, and then create his own experiments from those readings. The field of chemistry was changing because scientists were making one discovery after another. Some of the most important findings were the discoveries of elements such as aluminum and bromine.

The Basics of Chemistry

Chemistry is the science of matter. Matter is anything that takes up space or has a mass, while mass is the measure of the amount

Prior to the scientific revolution of the fifteenth and sixteenth centuries, the world of chemistry existed as alchemy. Alchemy is a science that deals with using chemicals to transform substances into other substances, particularly metals into gold. Alchemists also sought the answer to eternal life. Alchemy flourished for hundreds of years before the scientific revolution, when scientific experimentation replaced this ancient practice. In the wake of the revolution, several branches of science were born, including chemistry and biology. This 1937 painting by N. C. Wyeth captures a romantic image of alchemy, in which an old, wise alchemist works with an assistant in hopes of unraveling the mysteries of the universe.

of matter. Matter can be almost anything, from the tiniest grain of sand to an elephant to a planet.

Water is matter and so is air—because they both take up space. You cannot actually see air take up space, but you can see water take up space. You can simply fill a cup with water and see how water takes up space, or even look outside while it is raining and see raindrops and puddles. To visualize how air takes up space, think of blowing up a balloon. As you blow air into the balloon, the balloon inflates because air fills it up, taking up space.

States of Matter

You can see water whereas you cannot see air because water and air are in two different states of matter. Air is a gas and water is a liquid. There are three states of matter: solid, liquid, and gas. Water offers a great example of the three states of matter. When water is frozen, it becomes ice, the solid state of water. When ice melts, it becomes a liquid. When the liquid is boiled, the water turns to steam known as water vapor, the gaseous state of water.

Elements

Elements are the basic building blocks of all matter. They literally build everything around you. Nearly everything in the entire universe is created by different combinations of elements. There are more than 100 elements in total. Some common elements are oxygen, hydrogen, carbon, iron, and aluminum.

What Chemists Study

Chemists study matter to figure out what elements make up the matter. They pick a form of matter, then they study that matter until they figure out *exactly* what is in it. If a chemist is studying water, his or her first question will be: what elements make up water? He or she would then perform experiments by adding heat or electricity to the matter. Adding heat or cold is a good way to break down matter to its most basic ingredients, or its most basic elements.

From just this type of research, a chemist can isolate the elements that make up water. These experiments would show that water is made of two parts hydrogen and one part oxygen. This means water is a compound. A compound is a substance formed by two or more elements. In fact, hydrogen and oxygen are some of the most common elements found in the world. Now, can you see why finding a new element is such a huge discovery? Elements make everything!

Russia: Behind the Times

From late 1856 to early 1857, Mendeleyev taught at St. Petersburg University while working in the school's laboratories. But as his knowledge of chemistry grew, he became frustrated with Russia's place in the science world. Mendeleyev enjoyed teaching but had a hard time finding many Russian scientists who were performing more daring experiments that challenged the existing knowledge. Eventually, Mendeleyev began to see that Russia was lagging behind the rest of the world in science.

In the mid-1800s, Russia was still using an ancient calendar called the Julian calendar. The rest of world was using the Gregorian calendar, the one we still use today. This meant that Russia was twelve days behind the rest of the world! For example, when it was July 25, 1868, in France, it was only July 13, 1868, in

The Russian Academy of Sciences, located in St. Petersburg, is the country's leading institution for scientific research. The academy was founded in 1724, by Russian emperor Peter the Great (1625–1725). After its founding, Peter the Great invited scientists from around the world to study and research at the academy. From there, the academy flourished. By 1830, the academy had established several museums and zoos to allow for visiting scientists to do research. However, Russia's scientific community progressed at a much slower rate than the rest of the world, lagging behind other countries in scientific research. This would change in the last half of the nineteenth century.

Russia. Russia was behind the world in many other ways as well. The country was still using an old political system called feudalism, which places power in the hands of very few people and leaves most of the population very poor and unable to work toward a better life.

In terms of science, Russia had very little to offer Mendeleyev. While the rest of the world was booming with opportunities in chemistry, Russia did not have as many science-related jobs or science-oriented universities. Frustrated, Mendeleyev finally applied to study abroad for two years.

Off to Paris and Germany

In 1859, Mendeleyev received an opportunity to study with the renowned chemist Henri-Victor Regnault (1810–1878) in Paris, France. At the time, Regnault was one of the most important minds in the science world and was considered far ahead of his time. In physics, Regnault is best known for his careful measurements of the weight and density of many gases, liquids, and solids. For example, he was the first scientist to figure out that absolute zero is –459° Fahrenheit (–273° Celsius). Absolute zero is the zero point on the absolute temperature scale; –459.67°F (–273.15°C) or 0 Kelvin. It is the temperature at which molecular motion stops.

After studying with Regnault for a few months, Mendeleyev headed off to Heidelberg, Germany, to study with Robert Bunsen (1811–1899) and Gustav Kirchhoff (1824–1887). These two brilliant scientists were partners and shared a state-of-the-art laboratory. When Mendeleyev joined them, they were studying and developing a device called the spectroscope. This instrument helps scientists learn what elements make up a particular substance. The two scientists used their spectroscope to discover a new element, which they named rubidium. The spectroscope is still used today.

In the first few weeks of his visit, Mendeleyev spent long hours studying with Kirchhoff and Bunsen at their laboratory. Along with the spectroscope, Bunsen was working on a special burner to use during experiments. Today, we know this invention as the Bunsen burner, and it is still one of the most common laboratory tools. Just being around these two brilliant minds motivated Mendeleyev. Unfortunately, though, Mendeleyev was very moody and stubborn.

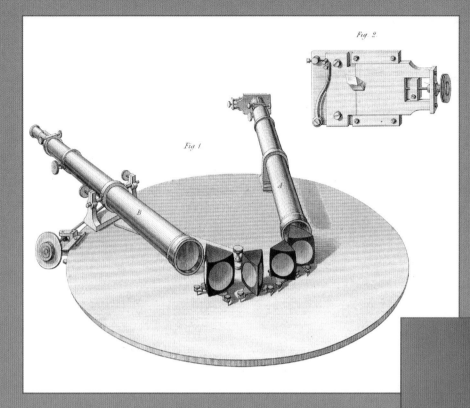

As a young man, Mendeleyev had the privilege to work alongside two other great minds, Robert Bunsen and Gustav Kirchhoff, both of whom made major contributions to the scientific world. Kirchhoff's spectroscope *(above)* can determine the chemical composition of matter by dispersing light into a spectrum, or a range of values. Bunsen created a burner that produced a constant flame. The Bunsen burner *(right)* would revolutionize the science lab, allowing for experiments to be performed over and over again without variation. While Mendeleyev and Bunsen later had a falling out, the competition between the two fueled Mendeleyev's desire to succeed.

As the weeks passed, Mendeleyev and Bunsen started to argue. At first, the pair only fought once in a while, but soon they were fighting every day. One day, in the middle of an argument, Mendeleyev stormed out of Bunsen and Kirchhoff's laboratory and vowed never to return.

Setting up His Own Laboratory

Mendeleyev's new lab in Heidelberg was nothing more than a small room jammed with lab equipment. In some ways, Mendeleyev had made a really bad decision when he walked out of Bunsen's laboratory. He was still quite young. He had learned a lot from these two scientists and still had much more to learn. However, Mendeleyev's bitterness toward his former mentor drove him to work exceptionally hard in his new home laboratory.

At first, Mendeleyev performed simple experiments on solubility—the amount of a substance that will dissolve in a given amount of another substance. He began working with alcohol and water. After a few experiments, Mendeleyev began to notice that his water and alcohol solutions shared some strong traits with gases such as hydrogen. He dug deeper, and soon Mendeleyev was studying elements and their valency. The valency of an atom is the measure of its ability to combine with other atoms. This would help determine how readily one atom combines with other atoms to form new substances. Soon Mendeleyev was publishing papers on his experiments with elements and valency. He suggested that figuring out an element's valency was just as important as figuring out its other physical and chemical properties. Many scientists agreed and turned their attention to valency.

A Great Mind for Science

Mendeleyev was a genius when it came to chemistry. He could not only remember a vast amount of complicated scientific information, but he could apply this information to come up with new ideas and experiments. Mendeleyev's mind worked in a constant process of trial and error. Each experiment he performed led him further. Many times, Mendeleyev's experiments were based on mere hunches, but these hunches came from his ability to think through complex scientific information. Mendeleyev's mind had a natural ability to see patterns. From these patterns, Mendeleyev built his experiments.

Eventually, at his home laboratory, Mendeleyev was able to reach new levels in his experiments. Oftentimes, after reading an interesting article on solutions (two or more liquid substances mixed together), he would then experiment in his lab, taking what he read even further. Mendeleyev reported his new findings in his own scientific article. When Mendeleyev worked, he became enthralled with his experiments. Although he was working with solutions, his experiments often led him back to the basic elements, which he would isolate from the original solution. As he performed more of these experiments, new patterns were beginning to emerge. As Mendeleyev worked, his mind began to gravitate toward the bigger picture, concluding that there must be some relationship between all the patterns. Mendeleyev was becoming more and more interested in classifying the elements. He wanted to know how they all fit together.

CHAPTER 3

After working in Germany for two years, Mendeleyev headed back to St. Petersburg in 1863. At age thirty, he accepted a job as professor of chemistry at the Technological Institute at St. Petersburg University. That same year, Mendeleyev married Feozva Lescheva.

Over the next two years, Mendeleyev worked incredibly hard at his job while he also worked toward his doctorate, or his Ph.D. A Ph.D. is the highest degree a person can earn in college. By 1865, Mendeleyev had earned his Ph.D. from St.

STEPS TO DISCOVERY

Petersburg University. A year later, he was named chairperson of the chemistry department at the university. This was a huge accomplishment for Mendeleyev. His professional life was going well and so was his personal life. He and his wife had their first child in 1866, a son they named Volodya. Soon after, they had a daughter they named Olga.

Hitting a New Scientific Key

By 1869, Mendeleyev had been teaching at the Technological Institute for six years. He had come into his own as a professor and furthered his reputation as a brilliant scientist. Mendeleyev's students loved him. He did not just teach chemistry, he made it fun. Mendeleyev enjoyed teaching, and it showed.

Mendeleyev's first part of *The Principles of Chemistry* was the major stepping stone on his path to discovering the periodic table of elements. After teaching at St. Petersburg University for several years, Mendeleyev realized he did not possess a textbook that could teach his students to properly understand the relationships between the elements. In the mid-1860s, Mendeleyev began writing a text that would meet these needs. The result was *The Principles of Chemistry*, which appeared in four parts. The first part appeared in 1868, the same year he became a founding member of the Russian Chemical Society. This 1901 edition was one of the first printings to include all four parts of Mendeleyev's groundbreaking work. (See page 55 for a transcription.)

A LIBRARY OF
UNIVERSAL LITERATURE

IN FOUR PARTS

Comprising Science, Biography, Fiction
and the Great Orations

PART ONE—SCIENCE

The Principles of Chemistry

(PART ONE)

BY
D. MENDELÉEFF

NEW YORK
P. F. COLLIER AND SON
·MCMI·
25

As a scientist, Mendeleyev published many articles on his experiments and many of his theories. In fact, during the mid-1860s, Mendeleyev had begun work on his first book, *The Principles of Chemistry*. After it was published, Mendeleyev saw the need for a second volume. At the time, however, Mendeleyev did not know that the second volume of *The Principles of Chemistry* would bring him face-to-face with something that would change the world of chemistry forever.

The Principles of Chemistry

Mendeleyev's *Principles of Chemistry* was his passion. Mendeleyev put every ounce of his knowledge into this book. As

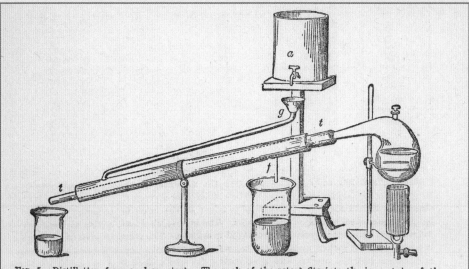

FIG. 5.—Distillation from a glass retort. The neck of the retort fits into the inner tube of the Liebig's condenser. The space between the inner and outer tube of the condenser is filled with cold water, which enters by the tube *g* and flows out at *f*.

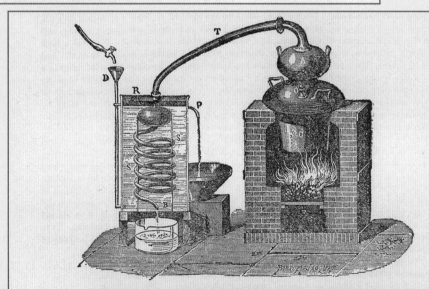

FIG. 4.—Distillation by means of a metallic still. The liquid in C is heated by the fire F. The vapours rise through the head A and pass by the tube T to the worm S placed in a vessel R, through which a current of cold water flows by means of the tubes D and P.

Much of Mendeleyev's inspiration was his desire to educate. One result from this desire was the four-part *Principles of Chemistry*. Like Mendeleyev's teaching career, *Principles* was not a boring text, but rather an engaging work that approached chemistry in a practical manner. Above are just two of the many illustrations that appear throughout the text. These illustrations demonstrate two ways chemists distilled water during the 1800s. Distilled water is often used in chemistry experiments because it is nearly pure water, without any foreign elements that could influence an experiment. (See page 55 for a transcription.)

Paul Strathern explains in *Mendeleyev's Dream: The Quest for the Elements*, Mendeleyev's *Principles of Chemistry* was one of the most important and detailed books published on chemistry during the time. *Principles* was so long that the book's footnotes—notes of reference, explanation, or comment usually placed below the text on a printed page—ended up as long as the book itself. Even though the book was so complex, it remained the most popular and definitive book on chemistry for more than thirty years.

By February 1869, Mendeleyev had already written the first volume of the book, and he was now working on *The Principles of Chemistry*'s second volume. Mendeleyev finished the first two chapters on alkali metal groups. Some alkali metals include sodium and potassium. However, chapter three posed a problem because before he could write it, he had to figure out what group of elements most resembled the alkali metal groups. He was stuck.

Organizing the Elements

When Mendeleyev sat down to write chapter three of *The Principles of Chemistry*'s second volume, he felt the pressure of his approaching self-imposed deadline. Mendeleyev had one last weekend to meet the deadline to complete chapter three. Unfortunately, he was going out of a town for a few days immediately after his deadline to give a lecture and to tour the Russian countryside. He knew he had to make a lot of progress on his book over the weekend, but he was feeling a little overwhelmed about how to continue.

One of the problems facing Mendeleyev was that he had noticed a big problem with the elements in the entire field of chemistry. By 1869, chemists had already discovered sixty elements. (Today, more

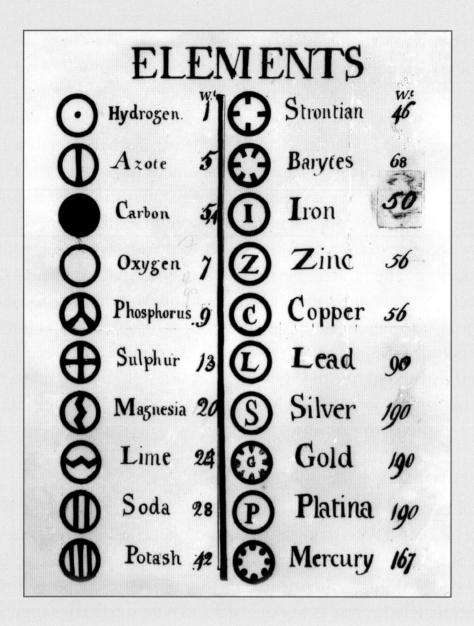

ELEMENTS

		w.t				w.t
⊙	Hydrogen.	1		Strontian		46
	Azote	5		Barytes		68
●	Carbon	54	I	Iron		50
○	Oxygen	7	Z	Zinc		56
	Phosphorus	9	C	Copper		56
⊕	Sulphur	13	L	Lead		90
	Magnesia	20	S	Silver		190
	Lime	24	g	Gold		190
	Soda	28	P	Platina		190
	Potash	42		Mercury		167

Many influences led to Mendeleyev's periodic table of elements. One was the work of English chemist John Dalton, who devised this table of elements in 1803. Dalton assigned the known elements chemical symbols and categorized them by their known atomic weights. While his symbols would soon be discarded, Dalton's atomic theory laid the groundwork for modern chemistry. In his theory, Dalton was the first to put forth the idea that all matter is made up of atoms. His theory also stated that atoms are indivisible and indestructible, and that compounds are combinations of two or more atoms.

SOME ELEMENTS DISCOVERED BY 1869

Aluminum (Al): Discovered in 1825 by Hans Ørsted in Denmark.

Boron (B): Discovered in 1808 by J. L. Gay-Lussac and L. J. Thenard in Paris, France, as well as Sir Humphry Davy in London, England.

Calcium (Ca): Discovered in 1808 by Sir Humphry Davy in London, England.

Carbon (C): Discovered by ancient civilizations.

Hydrogen (H): Discovered in 1766 by Henry Cavendish in London, England.

Iron (Fe): Discovered by ancient civilizations.

Lithium (Li): Discovered in 1817 by J. A. R. Arfvedson in Sweden.

Nitrogen (N): Discovered in 1772 by Daniel Rutherford in Edinburgh, Scotland.

Oxygen (O): Discovered around 1774 by Joseph Priestley in England.

Zinc (Zn): Known in India and China before 1500 and by the Greeks and Romans before 20 BC.

than 110 elements have been identified.) However, even though numerous scientists had identified so many elements over the years, there was no way to organize all the elements on a chart that demonstrated the relationships between the elements. Mendeleyev was well aware of this problem. He also knew he could not write chapter three of his book without first organizing the known elements.

Mendeleyev's deadline came and went, and his frustration only grew. He paced through his office, muttering, and thinking as hard as he could. Even his brilliant mind could not unlock the key to the elements. After a few hours, his office was a mess. There were papers everywhere. He had notes scribbled in the margins of books, on random pieces of paper, even in old notebooks he had used while a student at St. Petersburg University. He just could not figure out how to organize all of the elements. He was looking at his notes, his books, and other scientists' research. Finally, he realized that since no one else had come up with the answer, he would have to do it.

Researching the Key

With his mind made up, Mendeleyev devoted himself to figuring out how to organize all the elements. First, he knew he had to find a pattern—a pattern that tied all of the elements together. He found a paper written in 1862 on this topic by French geologist A. E. Béguyer de Chancourtois, who thought he had figured out part of the pattern. De Chancourtois had created a list of the elements arranged by increasing atomic weight. (Atomic weight is how much an element weighs.) De Chancourtois is credited with creating the first representation of the periodic law. The periodic law basically states that elements are grouped naturally, with each group having different characteristics, or properties, such as melting point, or phase at room temperature.

Unfortunately, de Chancourtois could not really explain the pattern he had found. He thought the elements could be grouped by their chemical properties. Chemical properties are the basic characteristics of how elements react with one another, such as hydrogen (H) and oxygen (O) bonding to form a water molecule (H_2O). Mendeleyev thought de Chancourtois was sort of on the right track. But Mendeleyev wondered about the physical properties. A physical property

German chemist Julius Lothar Meyer also devised an early model for organizing the elements, which he published in his 1864 book, *Die Moderne Theroien der Chemie* (Modern Theories of Chemistry). While Meyer and Mendeleyev had similar career paths, their routes to the world of chemistry were quite different. Mendeleyev came from humble beginnings, while Meyer was born into a family of physicians. In Meyer's 1864 work, his table of elements contained a tabulation of twenty-eight elements, indicating a valence (combining power) that occurs as atomic weight increases. Unlike Meyer's work, Mendeleyev's 1869 periodic table categorized all sixty-three of the known elements into an ordered chart. (See page 55 for a transcription.)

MODERN THEORIES

OF

CHEMISTRY

BY

DR LOTHAR MEYER

PROFESSOR OF CHEMISTRY IN THE UNIVERSITY OF TÜBINGEN

TRANSLATED FROM THE GERMAN (5TH EDITION)

BY

P. PHILLIPS BEDSON, D.Sc. (LOND.), B.Sc. (VICT.), F.C.S.

PROFESSOR OF CHEMISTRY IN THE DURHAM COLLEGE OF SCIENCE, NEWCASTLE-UPON-TYNE

AND

W. CARLETON WILLIAMS, B.Sc., F.C.S.

PROFESSOR OF CHEMISTRY IN THE FIRTH COLLEGE, SHEFFIELD

LONDON

LONGMANS, GREEN, AND CO.

AND NEW YORK : 15 EAST 16th STREET

1888

is just as it sounds: the physical traits of a substance, such as color, density, melting point, or boiling point.

Another Scientist on the Hunt

Meanwhile, English chemist John A. R. Newlands was also spending his time researching how to group the elements. Like de Chancourtois, he was concentrating on "wrapping" the elements. Wrapping the elements means he plotted the elements in a cylinder shape, literally wrapping them around cylindrical shapes to reflect their common traits. This shape would have overlaps, thus revealing how some elements shared properties. Of the sixty-three known elements, Newlands found that chemical

In February 1869, Mendeleyev knew he was on the doorstep of a major scientific breakthrough. His entire life's work had brought him to this moment, but there was one elusive piece missing from his puzzle. Mendeleyev created many different versions of the periodic table, mixing and matching elements until he devised a table that worked. Little did anyone know, an afternoon nap would provide the key to unlocking the mystery. Unknown to Mendeleyev, German chemist Julius Lothar Meyer was also close to completing a table that organized all the elements. Meyer had published a smaller, simple table in 1864 which classified elements into six families. Mendeleyev's 1869 table expanded on his earlier table.

groups—elements that share similar chemical properties (the same traits when reacting with other elements)—repeated every eight elements. He named this the octave rule and compared it to a musical scale.

With both of these scientists' research in mind, Mendeleyev began plotting out all the elements on a piece of paper. When his first version didn't make sense, he made a new version. Then he plotted a newer version and so on. Over the next two days, Mendeleyev designed more than ten different ways to organize the known elements. None of them worked.

CHAPTER 4

THE RIGHT ANSWER: EUREKA!

On February 17, 1869, after three days of testing different groupings, Mendeleyev was exhausted. He was so obsessed with figuring out how to group the elements that he had spent three whole days awake, working on a possible solution. During those three days, Mendeleyev had come up with very little.

On the morning of February 17, Mendeleyev decided to take a break for some breakfast. After eating, he returned to his study and opened a letter from the Voluntary Economic Cooperative of Tver. The letter detailed the trip he was to take that day—to give a lecture to factory workers, then visit the Russian countryside. He was supposed to leave on a train right after breakfast. This letter would soon become a piece of scientific history.

On the back of the letter, Mendeleyev had written down the atomic weights for four elements from the same group: fluorine (F), chlorine (Cl), bromine (Br), and iodine (I). These four elements are all part of the halogen group—meaning all of these elements share some physical and chemical properties. When Mendeleyev looked at what he wrote, he began to see a pattern. The elements could be grouped not only by atomic weight but by chemical property!

ELEMENTS AND THEIR SYMBOLS

Whenever a new element is discovered, scientists assign that element a symbol, or abbreviation. A scientific symbol is really just a shorter way of representing a longer, more complex word. For example, if a scientist is studying the element phosphorus, he or she would not want to write "phosphorus" every time he or she needed to identify the element. It is too long and takes too much time to write down. Therefore, phosphorus's symbol is P. Every single one of the elements has a symbol. Oxygen's symbol is O. Sulfur's symbol is S. Carbon's symbol is C. A few of them are trickier, such as Fe for Iron. These symbols can be used to represent the different elements found in various compounds, or combinations. For example, carbon monoxide—the dangerous chemical released from car exhaust—is written as CO. This tells you that carbon monoxide is made of one carbon (C) and one oxygen (O) atom.

Mendeleyev then did the same thing for another group of elements with similar chemical properties he called the oxygen group: oxygen (O), sulfur (S), selenium (Se), and tellurium (Te). Again, when Mendeleyev grouped them by their atomic weight, he saw a similar pattern. Of course, Mendeleyev was using each element's symbol when he was writing them down. His computations looked like this:

Chemical Symbol = Atomic Weight

F = 19	Cl = 35	Br = 80	I = 127
O = 16	S = 32	Se = 79	Te = 128

In 1869, this is how the world first glimpsed Mendeleyev's marvelous invention, the periodic table of elements. Like many great inventions, Mendeleyev's table was genius in its simplicity. Mendeleyev's table properly organized the elements and demonstrated their relationships with each other. The table also demonstrated the periodic law, which today states that properties of the elements recur periodically with increasing atomic number. Mendeleyev's original table would see many changes during the next century. (See page 56 for a transcription.)

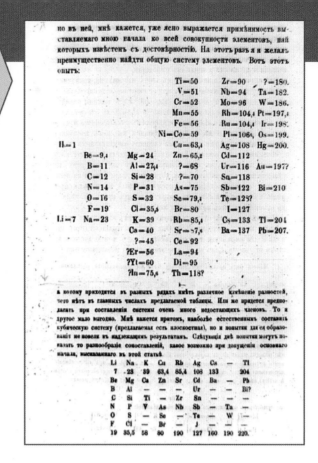

This simple chart showed a pattern when the elements were grouped by their atomic weight and by their similar properties. In Mendeleyev's earliest notes, almost all of the atomic weights get smaller going down the column. Also, the atomic weights get larger going across the rows. Mendeleyev noticed this pattern, and it gave him an idea.

The Eureka Moment

When Mendeleyev's friend A. Inostrantzev stopped by on the morning of February 17, he found the scientist working on his new chart. Inostrantzev also arrived to find his friend extremely frustrated and upset. Mendeleyev told Inostrantzev that he knew he was close to making a great discovery, but he just could not figure it out. How did the elements fit together?

By this time, Mendeleyev had missed his train to the countryside, but it did not matter. He knew that he was close and could

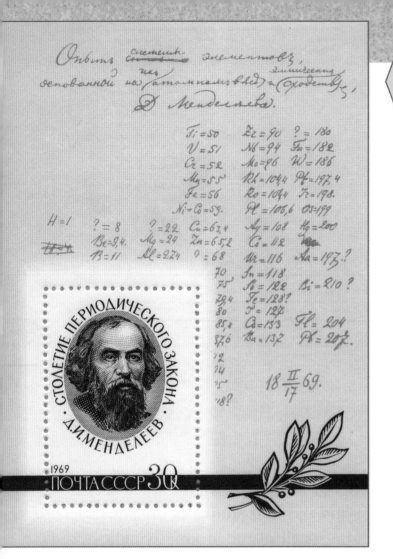

not stop now. As February 17 came to a close, Mendeleyev still had not come up with a way to organize the elements. His mind and body were overcome with fatigue, but he continued to work in his study, obsessed with finding the solution. As the night passed, Mendeleyev's body gave up on him. He fell asleep in his study, his head resting on his arms atop his desk.

In a deep sleep, Mendeleyev drifted into a dream. Then it happened. Mendeleyev figured it out! Later he recalled, "I saw in a dream a table where all the elements fell into place as required. Awakening, I immediately wrote it down on a piece of paper." In his dream, Mendeleyev saw the answer. He realized that when

DREAMING AND THINKING

Have you ever been told to get a good night's rest before a test? Today, scientific research shows that while a person is dreaming, he or she processes an enormous amount of information. Scientists believe that dreams are a way for a person to process his or her daily experiences. Research has shown that while asleep, the brain is still actively processing thoughts and emotions, including any information taken in during the day. In fact, during REM (rapid eye movement) sleep, the brain works on overdrive to process complex information. This ranges from decision making to learning how to do new things, such as playing a musical instrument. In Mendeleyev's case, his dreams gave way to an amazing discovery!

the elements were listed in order of their atomic weights, their chemical and physical properties repeated in a series.

The Periodic Table of Elements

For two weeks, Mendeleyev perfected his new creation. When he was satisfied with his new discovery, Mendeleyev published the periodic table of elements in a paper called "A Suggested System of the Elements." The title "periodic table" is used for the recurring properties that periodically occur between the elements, allowing them to be grouped together. The rows in Mendeleyev's table list the elements in order by their atomic weights, from smallest to largest. The vertical columns list the elements in groups with similar chemical and physical properties.

ПЕРИОДИЧЕСКАЯ СИСТЕМА ЭЛЕМЕНТОВ

ПЕРИОДЫ	РЯДЫ	I	II	III	IV	V	VI	VII	VIII			0
1	I	H 1 1,008										He 2 4,003
2	II	Li 3 6,940	Be 4 9,02	B 5 10,82	C 6 12,010	N 7 14,008	O 8 16,000	F 9 19,00				Ne 10 20,183
3	III	Na 11 22,997	Mg 12 24,32	Al 13 26,97	Si 14 28,06	P 15 30,98	S 16 32,06	Cl 17 35,457				Ar 18 39,944
4	IV	K 19 39,096	Ca 20 40,08	Sc 21 45,10	Ti 22 47,90	V 23 50,95	Cr 24 52,01	Mn 25 54,93	Fe 26 55,85	Co 27 58,94	Ni 28 58,69	
	V	Cu 29 63,57	Zn 30 65,38	Ga 31 69,72	Ge 32 72,60	As 33 74,91	Se 34 78,96	Br 35 79,916				Kr 36 83,7
5	VI	Rb 37 85,48	Sr 38 87,63	Y 39 88,92	Zr 40 91,22	Nb 41 92,91	Mo 42 95,95	Ma 43 —	Ru 44 101,7	Rh 45 102,91	Pd 46 106,7	
	VII	Ag 47 107,88	Cd 48 112,41	In 49 114,76	Sn 50 118,70	Sb 51 121,76	Te 52 127,61	J 53 126,92				Xe 54 131,3
6	VIII	Cs 55 132,91	Ba 56 137,36	La 57 ★ 138,92	Hf 72 178,6	Ta 73 180,88	W 74 183,92	Re 75 186,31	Os 76 190,2	Ir 77 193,1	Pt 78 195,23	
	IX	Au 79 197,2	Hg 80 200,61	Tl 81 204,39	Pb 82 207,21	Bi 83 209,00	Po 84 210	85 —				Rn 86 222
7	X	87 —	Ra 88 226,05	Ac 89 227	Th 90 232,12	Pa 91 231	U 92 238,07					

★ ЛАНТАНИДЫ 58–71

Ce 58 140,13	Pr 59 140,92	Nd 60 144,27	61 —	Sm 62 150,43	Eu 63 152,0	Gd 64 156,9
Tb 65 159,2	Dy 66 162,46	Ho 67 164,94	Er 68 167,2	Tu 69 169,4	Yb 70 173,04	Cp 71 174,99

Many chemists tried to organize the elements in the years prior to Mendeleyev's success. Mendeleyev succeeded because he was able to foresee that there existed a number of unknown elements with atomic weights that would fall between the weights of the known elements. Therefore, Mendeleyev left gaps in his final table. Once Mendeleyev published his table in 1869, it took many years for it to be widely accepted in the scientific community. Finally, in 1879, Mendeleyev's table earned the credibility it deserved following the discoveries of the elements gallium, germanium, and scandium. These elements fit into the exact empty spaces on the table, exactly where Mendeleyev predicted they would fit. This version of the periodic table was created in the late 1800s.

Gaps in the Periodic Table

Mendeleyev was so convinced his table was correct that he took it a step farther. In 1869, only sixty-three out of the more than 100 elements had been discovered. Brilliantly, Mendeleyev left room in his table for elements not yet discovered! For example, on Mendeleyev's original table, there is a gap

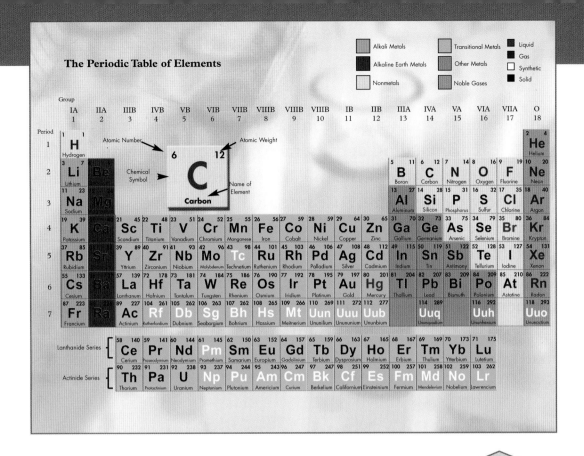

The Periodic Table of Elements

Today, the periodic table of elements is an integral part of classrooms and laboratories around the world. Today's periodic table is a direct descendant of Mendeleyev's original table. Over the years, the table has been tweaked and reorganized. The biggest change is that today's table is organized by atomic number, while Mendeleyev's table used atomic weight. Since Mendeleyev first published his table in 1869, more than forty elements have been added to the table. Scientists are still discovering elements today.

between Tl = 204 (thallium) and Bi = 208 (bismuth). Mendeleyev left this gap because he assumed new elements would be discovered and placed in this column with atomic weights of 205 through 207.

Then on November 29, 1870, Mendeleyev took his table even further. According to the American Physics Institute, Mendeleyev published a paper stating that it was possible to predict the properties of undiscovered elements. He then proceeded to make predictions for three new elements [aluminum, boron, and silicon] and suggested several properties of each, including density, radii, and combining ratios with oxygen, among others. Again, Mendeleyev was able to predict these new elements because he saw the gaps in his table. With more experiments, he was even more convinced that gaps in the table represented elements that had not yet been discovered. He was able to predict the properties by looking at the elements near the gap and making estimates.

Again, Mendeleyev was right. Just as he predicted, his original table would eventually be revised when new elements were discovered.

Understanding Mendeleyev's Discovery

Although Mendeleyev's periodic table is now regarded as a tremendous discovery, the table was met with disapproval following its formal publication in 1870. In fact, most scientists dismissed the table because they thought it was completely incorrect. Scientists looked at Mendeleyev's periodic table of elements and saw a theory with holes in it. They viewed the gaps that Mendeleyev intentionally included in the table as mistakes or things Mendeleyev was unable to explain. At first, Mendeleyev's amazing discovery was not even considered a legitimate idea.

Further Investigations and Research

Mendeleyev was not put off by other scientists' disbelief. In fact, the disapproval made him research his theory even more. As Mendeleyev did more research, all of his findings supported the fact that his table was absolutely correct. However, even though Mendeleyev published more papers on why his periodic table of elements was correct, scientists still did not believe his findings.

Just a year after Mendeleyev published his table, a German scientist named Julius Lothar Meyer (1830–1895), who was working independently of Mendeleyev, published a table very similar to Mendeleyev's periodic table of elements. Today, Mendeleyev is given credit for the periodic table of elements because he published his findings first. At the time, though, Meyer's paper lent some validity to Mendeleyev's table. However, it still did not offer enough for scientists to accept the periodic table of elements.

Mendeleyev spent the next five years researching his table. With each experiment, he further confirmed that his periodic table of elements was indeed correct. The only question that remained was, when was the rest of science going to catch on?

CHAPTER 5

CHEMISTRY COMES OF AGE

In November 1875, Mendeleyev's great discovery finally got the recognition it deserved. When French chemist Paul-Émile Lecoq de Boisbaudran (1838–1912) discovered one of the missing elements, which he named gallium (Ga), Mendeleyev's predictions about the missing elements were proven true. Interestingly, this moment almost did not happen, and Mendeleyev's table might have been thrown out altogether. A year later, Lecoq de Boisbaudran published a paper showing Mendeleyev's predictions. In it, Lecoq de Boisbaudran said that the specific gravity of gallium was 4.7, whereas Mendeleyev's table predicted it would have a specific gravity of 5.9. (Mendeleyev had named this element aluminum.) So, how did Lecoq de Boisbaudran's work contradict Mendeleyev's theory? Lecoq de Boisbaudran actually made a mistake during his research. His one little miscalculation led to an entirely different result, leading him to conclude that Mendeleyev's table did not work.

When Mendeleyev read the paper, he immediately wrote a long letter to Lecoq de Boisbaudran, asking him to redo his experiment. At first Lecoq de Boisbaudran refused, saying that Mendeleyev, in fact, was the one who was wrong. A few months later, Lecoq de Boisbaudran conducted the experiment again

Like many other minds in the world of science, Mendeleyev has other scientists to thank for pushing him to succeed and bring his great invention to the world. After Mendeleyev published his first periodic table in 1869, French chemist Paul Emile Lecoq de Boisbaudran published work that seemed to disprove Mendeleyev's work. Less determined men might have given up. Mendeleyev, however, was driven to prove his periodic table was the correct one. In 1875, Lecoq de Boisbaudran discovered a new element he named gallium. The new element fit onto the periodic table exactly where Mendeleyev predicted it would. Lecoq de Boisbaudran would go on to discover the elements Samarium (1880) and dysprosium (1886).

and found that Mendeleyev was right. The specific gravity of gallium was, in fact, 5.9. Lecoq de Boisbaudran then published a new paper that supported Mendeleyev's periodic table of elements. Finally, the world of science had caught up.

Rising to the Top

When Lecoq de Boisbaudran published his paper, Mendeleyev's career skyrocketed. Seemingly overnight, Mendeleyev was instantly considered a genius. Likewise, demand for him to write and lecture about the periodic table of elements was incredible. Science associations around the world wanted Mendeleyev to speak at their conferences while numerous universities offered him honorary degrees. Mendeleyev was at the top; he felt very proud of his work as he was finally being recognized for his amazing discovery.

By 1880, Mendeleyev's periodic table was being used all over the world. Like many great scientific discoveries, Mendeleyev's table pushed other chemists even further, encouraging more and more exploration in the world of chemistry. The gaps on Mendeleyev's table spurred scientists into action, sparking a massive search for the missing elements.

In 1880, a discovery by German scientist Clemens Winkler (1838–1904) again showed the brilliance of the periodic table of elements. When Winkler discovered a new element, which he named germanium (Ge), the element's atomic weight matched perfectly with a missing piece in Mendeleyev's table. Again, the science world was shown that Mendeleyev's table was the real thing!

Over the course of the next twenty years, Mendeleyev's periodic table of elements served as a guide for the discovery of many new elements, including argon (Ar) as well as twenty others. Then in 1898, Marie Curie (1867–1934) made a huge discovery when she discovered radium (Ra). Curie's work was one of the most pioneering because it led to a better understanding of radioactive energies and materials.

Divorce and Marriage

As Mendeleyev's career skyrocketed, his marriage began to fall apart. He and his wife had never really been close, and now with Mendeleyev's tours and speaking engagements, they rarely saw one another. In 1882, Mendeleyev divorced his wife, Feozva. Only a few months later, Mendeleyev remarried a woman named Ann Popova. The new couple eventually had four children together.

Mendeleyev's periodic table would provide a map that would allow later scientists to unravel some of the world's greatest mysteries. One such mystery is the world of subatomic particles. Mendeleyev's table categorized the elements correctly and demonstrated elements' relationships with the others on the table. However, the reasons for these relationships lay in subatomic particles. Soon electrons, protons, and neutrons were discovered. These subatomic particles further explained the relationships among the elements. Research into subatomic particles would eventually lead to the discovery of DNA and the creation of nuclear energy.

New Sciences Explode

When Mendeleyev published the periodic table of elements, he was inspired by his discovery. He saw his contribution to chemistry as a launching pad to many other discoveries, and it was. Today Mendeleyev's table is still the basis of modern chemistry. The periodic table ultimately gave way to major discoveries in many areas of science.

Discovery of Subatomic Particles

In Mendeleyev's day, the atom was considered the most basic particle of matter. An atom is the smallest particle of an element that can exist either alone or in combination. Scientists believed that an atom could not be broken down any further. However, Mendeleyev's periodic table made scientists rethink this idea. Only a few years after Mendeleyev's periodic table was published, scientists found that atoms contained smaller parts called subatomic particles. These subatomic particles—electrons, protons, and neutrons—are the building blocks of atoms. Mendeleyev had hoped that his table would pave the way to a better understanding of chemistry, and it did. Subatomic particles are the foundation of all elements, so through research, scientists had uncovered an even deeper understanding of chemistry.

A New Science

When scientists began researching subatomic particles, they realized that an entirely new branch of science was needed to study these small particles. They named this new branch of science nuclear physics. Nuclear physics is a branch of physics that includes the study of the subatomic particles of atoms and their interactions with each other.

Other Discoveries Made Possible by the Periodic Table

Mendeleyev's periodic table also inspired other fields of science, such as biology. Biology is the branch of science that studies living organisms, which can be anything from bacteria to plants to humans. The periodic table, and its illustration of elemental relationships, inspired scientists to begin research on what would later become one the most important discoveries in biology—deoxyribonucleic acid, or DNA, the building block of life. In 1953, James Watson (1928–) and Francis Crick (1916–2004) discovered that the DNA molecule twisted in the shape of a double

MENDELEYEV'S LEGACY

Mendeleyev's periodic table was deeply inspirational to the scientific world, and scientists everywhere appreciate his work. To show their appreciation and respect, many associations and universities have named things after Mendeleyev, honoring the man who created the periodic table of elements. The following is a small list of places and things dedicated to Mendeleyev's achievements as a scientist.

- Element 101, mendelevium (Md)
- Asteroid No. 2769 Mendeleev
- Russian Scientific Ship named the *Dmitry Mendeleev*
- Russian Mendeleev Chemical Society
- *Mendeleev Communications* (A magazine published jointly by the Royal Society of Chemistry and the Russian Academy of Science)
- *Mendeleev Chemistry Journal* (Abstracts in English)
- Mendeleyev University of Chemical Technology
- Mendeleev (A town in the suburbs of Moscow)
- Mendeleev Streets in Moscow and St. Petersburg
- Monument to Mendeleev in St. Petersburg

* List compiled by Moscow State University

helix, which is like a ladder twisted into a spiral. A DNA molecule contains all the hereditary information about the living organism that contains it—DNA plays a major role in controlling the activities of all cells in that organism. DNA decides who or what you are. It decides your hair color, your eye color, how tall you will be—everything!

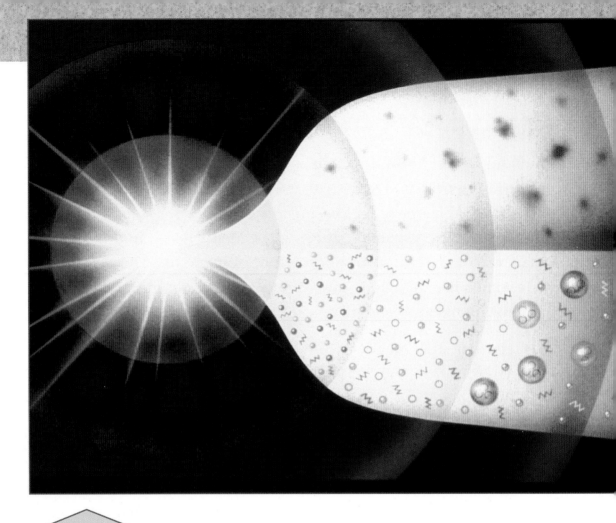

Many scientists attribute the origin of our universe to the big bang theory, which first arose in the early 1900s. The theory states that around 12 to 15 billion years ago, an explosion of matter created the universe. From this initial explosion, the universe has developed in stages. Immediately following the big bang, the universe formed from a mixture of particles. Soon protons and neutrons were formed. Once the universe cooled some 300,000 years later, atoms began to form. In the seventh stage, nearly 500 million years after the big bang, stars were born as well as the heavy elements. From there, life as we know it today began to develop.

How the Universe Began

Mendeleyev's periodic table even pushed scientists to inquire about how the universe began. They thought that if the elements could be organized and explained in a logical matter, so could everything else—even the origins of the universe. In the early

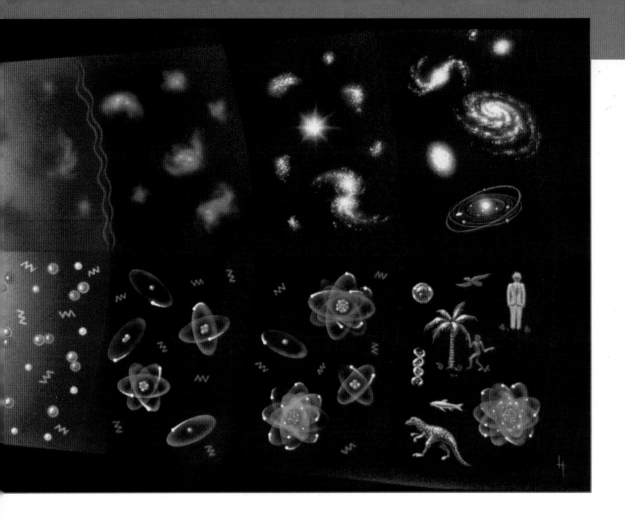

1900s, a theory emerged called the big bang theory. The theory states that the universe began when all matter and energy concentrated to a very high density and temperature some 12 to 15 billion years ago. The universe expanded from that small mass billions of years ago. In fact, the universe is still expanding to this day.

Mendeleyev's Perspective

Throughout the remainder of his career and life, Mendeleyev received many awards from various organizations. His *Principles of Chemistry* was awarded the Demidov Prize, one of the highest awards in Russia for educational texts. In 1882, Mendeleyev was also awarded the Davy Medal from the Royal Society of England, the country's oldest and most distinguished scientific association. Later in 1905, the society also gave

Dmitry Mendeleyev lived an inspirational life. From his poor childhood in remote Siberia, Mendeleyev eventually established himself as one of the world's great minds. This painting by Ilya Repin captures Mendeleyev near the end of his career, dressed in professorial robes after accepting one of many honorary degrees bestowed upon him. Few have contributed as much to science and our understanding of the universe as Mendeleyev has. Mendeleyev's periodic table of elements is found in nearly every science classroom around the world.

Mendeleyev the Copley Medal, the society's highest award. Both medals are awarded to those responsible for great scientific achievement.

Leaving St. Petersburg University

In 1890, when Mendeleyev was nearly sixty years old, he retired from his teaching position at the St. Petersburg University. By then, he had been a part of the university for more than forty years, since he was a student there. According to the Woodrow Wilson National Fellowship Foundation, Mendeleyev said in his last lecture at the university: "I have achieved an inner freedom. There is nothing in this world that I fear to say. No one nor anything can silence me. This is a good feeling. This is the feeling of a man. I want you to have this feeling too—it is my moral responsibility to help you achieve this inner freedom. I am an evolutionist of a peaceable type. Proceed in a logical and systematic manner."

After retiring from the university, the Russian government hired Mendeleyev as the director of the Bureau of Weights and Measures, which monitors and assists scientific research and programs. He remained an active and popular figure in the world of science until his death. Mendeleyev passed away on February 2, 1907, at the age of seventy-two. He died while sitting in his home in St. Petersburg, listening to Jules Verne's *Journey to the North Pole*, which was airing on the radio.

Mendeleyev's Gift to Education

At the young age of twenty Dmitry Mendeleyev published his first scientific article called "Chemical Analysis of a Sample from Finland." This article was to be the first mark of an amazing scientist. By the end of his career, Mendeleyev had written more than 250 science articles, which appeared in journals and science magazines. In addition, he wrote two books, *Organic Chemistry* and *The Principles of Chemistry*, both of which are regarded as two of the most important books science has ever produced.

In 1906, one year before his death, Mendeleyev published "A Project for a School for Teachers" and "Toward Knowledge of Russia." Both articles highlight two of Mendeleyev's deepest passions that he carried throughout his entire life: education and his homeland of Russia. To Mendeleyev, education was one of the most important areas in life. Teaching was a way to share his passion for science and enlighten future generations. Mendeleyev's career shows that education is important because it was only through hard work, research, and education that he constructed the periodic table of elements, his most incredible discovery.

In the early twentieth century, the periodic table experienced two major changes. One was the discovery of noble gases, such as helium (He) and neon (Ne). The second change came in 1914, when English physicist Henry Gwyn Jeffreys Moseley proved that arranging the element could be improved if they were arranged by atomic number. This change was slight, and simply swapped a few elements on the table.

Today, the periodic table of elements is revised as each new element is discovered. But even today's periodic table bears a striking resemblance to Mendeleyev's original table. More than 130 years old, Mendeleyev's table is still the foundation of modern chemistry. The table is found in nearly every chemistry classroom and laboratory in the entire world.

TIMELINE

February 8, 1834	Dmitry Ivanovich Mendeleyev is born in Tobolsk, Siberia, Russia.
1847	Mendeleyev's grades in school improve, and his teachers proclaim him brilliant.
1848–1850	Mendeleyev's father dies; the Mendeleyev family's glass factory burns down. They relocate to St. Petersburg, Russia. Mendeleyev enrolls in the Central Pedagogic Institute of St. Petersburg to study science.
1854	Mendeleyev publishes his first scientific article called "Chemical Analysis of a Sample from Finland."
1859	Mendeleyev studies with Henri-Victor Regnault in Paris and then studies with Robert Bunsen and Gustav Kirchhoff in Germany.
1859–1861	Mendeleyev sets up a home laboratory and publishes many papers on his experiments with solutions.
1863–1865	Mendeleyev becomes professor of chemistry at the Technological Institute in St. Petersburg; in 1865, receives his Ph.D. in chemistry.
1869	Mendeleyev finishes the first volume of his book *The Principles of Chemistry* and begins the second volume.

February 15–17, 1869	— For three days, Mendeleyev works on how to group the elements. On the third day, he dreams about the solution to the periodic table. He publishes his table in his second volume of *The Principles of Chemistry* later that year.
March 6, 1869	— A formal presentation of Mendeleyev's work is given to the Russian Chemical Society.
1870s	— Mendeleyev's table is challenged by the scientific community.
1880	— A discovery by Clemens Winkler affirms Mendeleyev's periodic table.
December 1882	— Mendeleyev receives the Davy Medal from the Royal Society of England.
1890	— Mendeleyev retires from St. Petersburg University. Russian government appoints him director of the Bureau of Weights and Measures.
1905	— Mendeleyev receives the Copley Medal from the Royal Society of England; receives honorary degrees from universities around the world.
February 2, 1907	— Mendeleyev dies at his home in St. Petersburg.

PRIMARY SOURCE TRANSCRIPTIONS

Page 25: The title page from Dmitry Mendeleyev's *The Principles of Chemistry*:

A Library of Universal Literature
In Four Parts
Comprising Science, Biography, Fiction and the Great Orations

Part One – Science

The Principles of Chemistry
(Part One)

by D. Mendeléeff

New York
P. F. Collier and Son
MCMI

Page 26: Two captions for illustrations from an English translation of Mendeleyev's *The Principles of Chemistry*.

(Top) Distillation from a glass retort. The neck of the retort fits into the inner tube of the Leibig's condenser. The space between the inner and outer tube of the condenser is filled with cold water, which enters by the tube g and glows out at f.

(Bottom) Distillation by means of a metallic still. The liquid in C is heated by the fire F. The vapours rise through the head A and pass by the tube T to the worm S placed in a vessel R, through which a current of cold water flows by means of the tubes D and P.

Page 31: Cover page for Julius Lothar Myer's book, *Die Moderne Theorien der Chemie* (Modern Theories of Chemistry).

Modern Theories of Chemistry
By
Dr. Lothar Meyer
Professor of Chemistry in the University of Tübingen
Translated from the German (5th Edition)
By
P. Philips Bedson, D.Sc. (Lond.), B.Sc. (Vict.), F.C.S.
Professor of chemistry in the Durham College of Science, Newcastle-upon-Tyne
And
W. Carleton Williams, B.Sc., F.C.S.
Professor of chemistry in the Firth College, Sheffield

London
Longmans, Green, and Co.
And New York: 15 East 16th Street
1888

Page 35: Transcription of a page from Mendeleyev's *The Principles of Chemistry*, 1869.

Section 1:

It is my conjecture that based upon the initial distribution of elements it is possible to determine, derive, the remaining elements of our universe. Based on this premise it is also possible to find a system for the entire spectrum of elements.

Section 2:

Elements are arranged according to groups where they share similar characteristics, and those properties in which they differ. The elements in the periodic table will be designated Roman numerals for classification.

The elements, for usefulness, should be depicted in a two dimensional plane. A three dimensional model would not serve well to demonstrate elemental configurations. The next two examples will illustrate variations in which exceptions exist.

GLOSSARY

alchemy A medieval chemical science and philosophy primarily aimed at turning metals into gold and the search for everlasting life.

atomic number The number of protons in the nucleus of an atom.

atomic weight The amount that one atom of an element weighs.

chemistry The study of matter and the changes that take place with that matter.

compound A substance formed by two or more elements.

elements The basic building blocks of all matter; a substance that cannot be broken down into simpler substances through ordinary chemistry.

footnote A note of reference, explanation, or comment usually placed below the text on a printed page.

force A "push" or "pull" experienced by a mass.

mass The measure of the amount of matter.

matter Anything that takes up space or has a mass.

Ph.D. Doctor of philosophy; the highest degree awarded by a graduate school.

physics The study of matter, motion, energy, and force.

prestigious Having a commanding position in people's minds.

refrain To keep oneself from doing or feeling something.

scholarship A grant, or financial aid, awarded to a student.

solution Two or more liquid substances that are mixed together.

valence The combining power of an element.

FOR MORE INFORMATION

American Association for the Advancement of Science (AAAS)
1200 New York Ave. NW
Washington, DC 20005
(202) 326-6400
e-mail: webmaster@aaas.org
Web site: http://www.aaas.org/

American Chemical Society (ACS)
1155 Sixteenth St. NW
Washington, DC 20036
(800) 227-5558
e-mail: webmaster@acs.org
Web site: http://www.chemistry.org/portal/a/c/s/1/home.html

American Institute of Physics
1 Physics Ellipse
College Park, MD 20740-3843
(301) 209-3100
e-mail: aipinfo@aip.org
Web site: http://www.aip.org/

Chemical Institute of Canada
130 Slater St., Ste. 550
Ottawa, ON K1P 6E2
(613) 232-6252
e-mail: info@cheminst.ca
Web site: http://www.cheminst.ca/

SCI America
177 Terrace Dr.
Chatham, NJ 07928
(973) 635-0189
e-mail: SCIAmerica@soci.info
Web site: http://www.soci.org/SCI/general/2001/html/ge120.jsp

The Society of Chemical Industry
14/15 Belgrave Ave.
London SW1X 8PS, UK
44 (0) 20 7598 1500
e-mail: secretariat@soci.org
Web site: http://www.soci.org/SCI/general/2001/html/ge120.jsp

Web Sites

Due to the changing nature of Internet links, the Rosen
Publishing Group, Inc., has developed an online list of Web
sites related to the subject of this book. This site is updated
regularly. Please use this link to access the list:

http://www. rosenlinks.com/psrsdt/mept

FOR FURTHER READING

Gordin, Michael. *A Well-Ordered Thing: Dmitrii Mendeleev and the Shadow of the Periodic Table*. New York: Basic Books, 2004.

Hasan, Heather. *Understanding the Elements of the Periodic Table: Iron*. New York: The Rosen Publishing Group, 2004.

Horvitz, Leslie Alan. *Eureka!: Stories of Scientific Discovery*. New York: John Wiley & Sons, Inc., 2002.

Kahn, Jetty. *Women in Chemistry Careers*. Mankato, MN: Capstone Books, 2000.

Meiani, Antonella. Translated by Maureen Spurgeon. *Chemistry*. Minneapolis, MN: Lerner Publishing Co., 2003.

Saucerman, Linda. *Understanding the Elements of the Periodic Table: Hydrogen*. New York: The Rosen Publishing Group, 2004.

Strathern, Paul. *Mendeleyev's Dream: The Quest for the Elements*. New York: Thomas Dunne Books, 2001.

BIBLIOGRAPHY

Allrefer.com Reference. "Transformation of Russia in the Nineteenth Century." Retrieved January 23, 2004 (http://reference.allrefer.com/country-guide-study/russia/russia23.html).

American Institute of Physics. "The Periodic Table of Elements." Retrieved January 25, 2003 (http://www.aip.org/history/curie/periodic.htm).

Andrew Rader Studios. "Rader's Chem4Kids." Retrieved January 25, 2004 (http://www.chem4kids.com).

Babaev, Eugene V. Moscow State University. "Dmitry Mendeleev Online." Retrieved January 25, 2004 (http://www.chem.msu.su/eng/misc/mendeleev/welcome.html).

Bucknell University. "Russia in the Nineteenth Century." Retrieved January 14, 2004 (http://www.departments.bucknell.edu/russian/fn9015/1800Russ.html).

Giroud, Vincent. "St. Petersburg: A Portrait of a Great City." Yale University. Retrieved January 25, 2004 (http://www.library.yale.edu/beinecke/petersburgex.htm).

Heilman, Chris. "The Pictorial Periodic Table." Retrieved January 25, 2004 (http://chemlab.pc.maricopa.edu/periodic/about.html).

Strathern, Paul. *Mendeleyev's Dream: The Quest for the Elements*. New York: Thomas Dunne Books, 2001.

WorldHealth.Net. "Dreams Essential for Processing Memories." From *Science* 2001; 294:1052-1057. Retrieved March 3, 2004 (http://www.worldhealth.net/p/237,268.html).

Zephyrus Interactive Education on the Web. "Dimitri Ivanovitch Mendeleyev." Retrieved January 25, 2004 (http://www.zephyrus.co.uk/dimitrimendeleev.html).

PRIMARY SOURCE IMAGE LIST

On the cover: A 1904 photomechanical print of Dmitry Mendeleyev by F. I. Blumbach.

Page 5: A photogravure after a photograph of Dmitry Mendeleyev taken in 1905, and first published in 1910 by Photographische Gessellschaft, Berlin, Germany.

Page 7: Photograph of young Dmitry Mendeleyev circa 1855. Housed at the Schoenberg Center for Electronic Text & Image, University of Pennsylvania, Philadelphia, PA.

Page 11: Photograph of Nevski Prospect, St. Petersburg, Russia. Housed at North Wind Picture Archives, Alfred, Maine.

Page 16: A 1937 oil-on-canvas painting laid down on board by N. C. Wyeth.

Page 21 (top): Illustration of a spectroscope, 1861, taken from the book *Unterschungen uber das Sonnenspectrum und die Spectren der chemischen Elemente*, by Gustav Kirchhoff and Robert Bunsen.

Page 21 (bottom): Photograph of an 1855 Bunsen burner.

Page 25: Title page from a 1901 edition of *The Principles of Chemistry* by Dmitry Mendeleyev, published by P. F. Collier and Son, New York.

Page 26: Two illustrations from the 1901 edition of *The Principles of Chemistry* by Dmitry Mendeleyev, published by P. F. Collier and Son, New York.

Page 28: John Dalton's table of elements of 1803, illustrating his atomic theory. Later published in *New System of Chemical Philosophy*, 1908.

Page 31: A folded leaf of plates by Julius Lothar Meyer, 1884.

Page 32: An unknown artist's portrait after a photograph of Dmitry Mendeleyev taken in 1900.

Page 35: Entitled "First Periodic Table of Chemical Elements Demonstrating the Periodic Law," first published in *The Principles of Chemistry*, 1869.

Page 43: Photograph of Paul-Émile Lecoq de Boisbaudran, housed at the University of Pennsylvania, Philadelphia, PA.

Page 50: Watercolor on paper portrait of Dmitry Mendeleyev by Ilya Repin, 1885.

INDEX

Credits

Cover, title page, pp. 5, 7, 43 Edgar Fahs Smith Collection, University of Pennsylvania Library; p. 11 North Wind Picture Archives; p. 14 The Art Archive/Scots Guards/Harper Collins Publishers; p. 16 *The Alchemist* by N. C. Wyeth. Courtesy the Chemical Heritage Foundation Collections, Philadelphia, Pennsylvania, USA. Photograph by Will Brown; p. 19 Universitetskaya Naberezhnaya, St. Petersburg, Russia/Bridgeman Art Library; p. 21 (top) Science Museum/Science & Society Picture Library; p. 21 (bottom) The Art Archive/Ara Collection Paris/Dagli Orti; pp. 25, 26, 31 Science, Industry and Business Library, The New York Public Library, Astor, Lenox, and Tilden Foundation; p. 28 © Bettmann/Corbis; p. 32 Time Life Pictures/Getty Images; p. 35 Library of Congress Prints and Photographs Collection; p. 38 © Sovfoto/Eastfoto; p. 39 by Tahara Hasan; p. 45 Mehau Kulyk/Photo Researchers, Inc.; pp. 48–49 David A. Hardy/Photo Researchers, Inc.; p. 50 Scala/Art Resource, NY.

Acknowledgments

Special thanks to translators Yuriy Karpinskyy and Eduard Riybovsky.

About the Author

Katherine White is a freelance writer and editor in and around New York City. She lives in Jersey City, New Jersey.

Editor: Charles Hofer; Photo Researcher: Rebecca Anguin-Cohen